THE ULTIMATE BUMPER STICKER BOOK

96 STICKERS FOR LOCKERS, NOTEBOOKS, & MORE!

I've seen normal
IT AIN'T PRETTY

EVERYBODY JUST CHILL

I don't do decaf

Don't make me use

UPPERCASE

WHATEVER

I'LL TRY TO BE NICER

IF YOU'LL TRY TO BE SMARTER

NEVER BELIEVE
GENERALIZATIONS

SHUT UP
and strap in

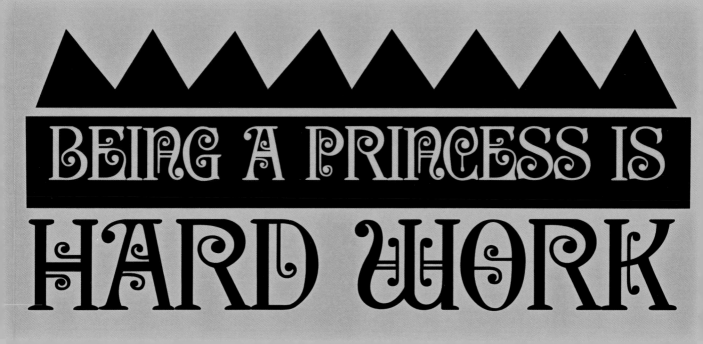

STOP VANDALISM

INSUFFICIENT MEMORY

The Dog Ate It. HONEST.

SATURDAY has a mOrninG?

Traumarama

MAKE IT STOP

CHOCOLATE

IT'S THE RIGHT ANSWER TO EVERY QUESTION

TALKING TO YOU IS A TOTAL WASTE OF MAKEUP

Are YOU necessary?

don't lie to kiDs

IF YOU'RE NOT OUTRAGED YOU'RE NOT PAYING ATTENTION

IT'S BEEN LOVELY BUT I HAVE TO

SCREAM NOW

NO COMMENT

EARTH
NOT MACHINE WASHABLE

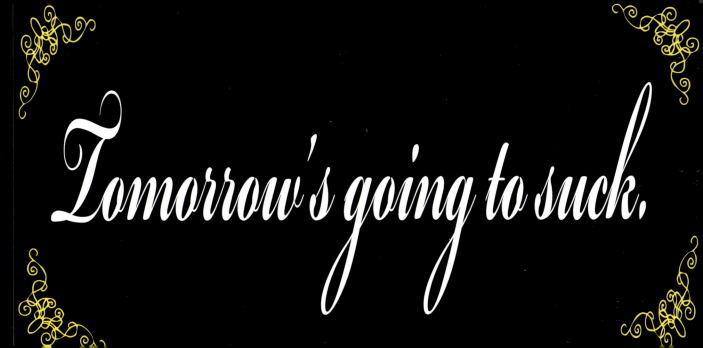

100%
CLUELESS

REBEL
without a clue

EVERYONE

is entitled to my opinion

I BET YOU HAVE A BLACK BELT IN STUPID

I see stupid people

I KNOW

what's best for you.

How
about a big
hot cup of

My Mood Ring Says

BACK OFF!

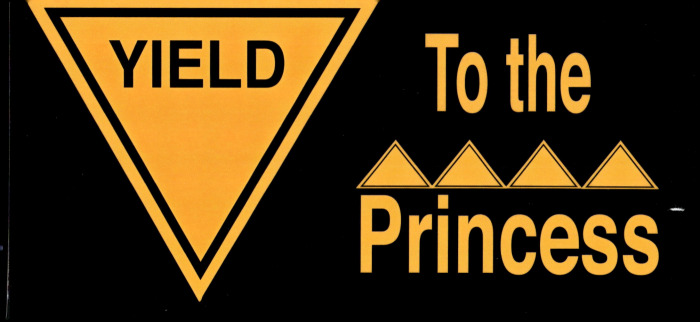

I DIDN'T SAY IT WAS YOUR FAULT

BUT I DID SAY TO BLAME YOU

IF YOU WANT MY RESPECT GET ON YOUR KNEES AND BEG FOR IT

A CLEAN DESK IS THE SIGN OF A CLUTTERED DRAWER

BATTERIES
NOT INCLUDED

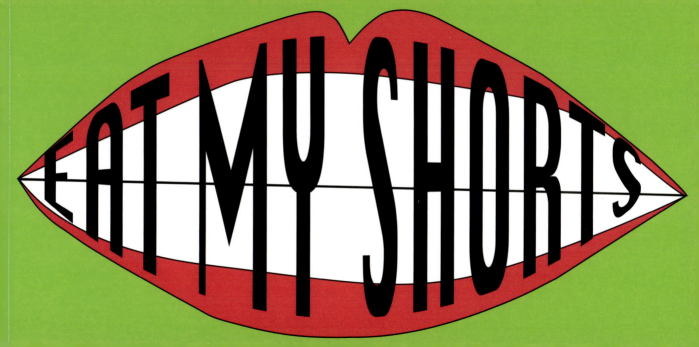

The more you

LISTEN

The more you know

GETTING ON YOUR FEET

MEANS

GETTING OFF YOUR BUTT

The road to success is always under construction

I'm not good at empathy

Would you settle for sarcasm?

And your point is?

IF IT'S TOO LOUD YOU'RE TOO OLD

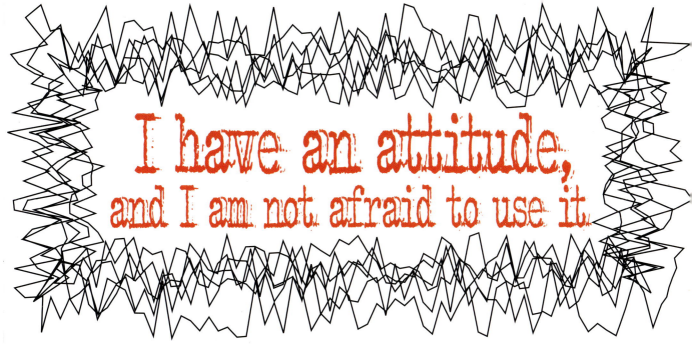

I have an attitude, and I am not afraid to use it

I WANT YOU TO STAY FAR, FAR AWAY

Don't rub the lamp unless you're ready for the genie

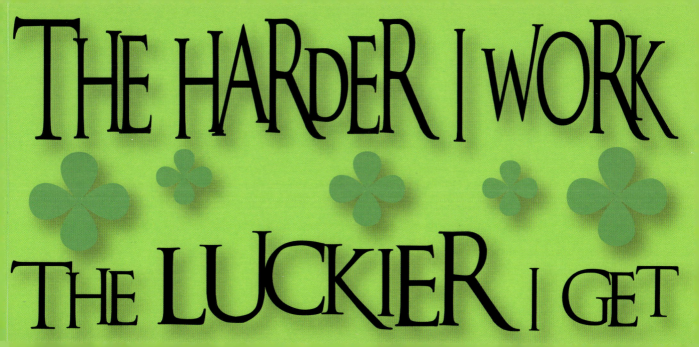

Don't make up your mind until you have one.

Where's HANNIBAL LECTER WHEN YOU NEED HIM?

SCHOOL'S OUT FOREVER!

ANOTHER BRILLIANT MIND RUINED BY EDUCATION

I'm not as stupid as you look

Please BE STUPID Somewhere Else

GET A LIFE

NO, NOT THIS ONE, ANOTHER ONE.

This would be funny if it weren't happening to me

please speak s-l-o-w-l-y

I don't speak IDIOT

I WILL TOLERATE YOU

I left the womb for this?

RELISH TODAY KETCHUP TOMORROW

ACTUAL SIZE

THIS IS THE
REBEL BASE

IF YOU'RE HAPPY AND YOU KNOW IT
keep it to yourself

CAUTION: *HOT!*

Reduce Greenhouse Gases:

DON'T EXHALE

CHANGE IS GOOD

you go first

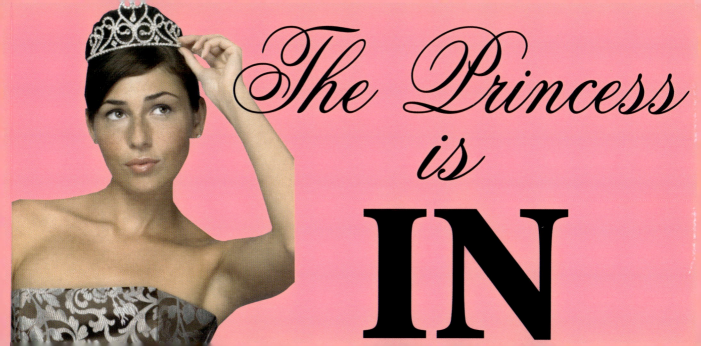

ENOUGH!

DID YOU EAT AN EXTRA BOWL OF STUPID THIS MORNING?

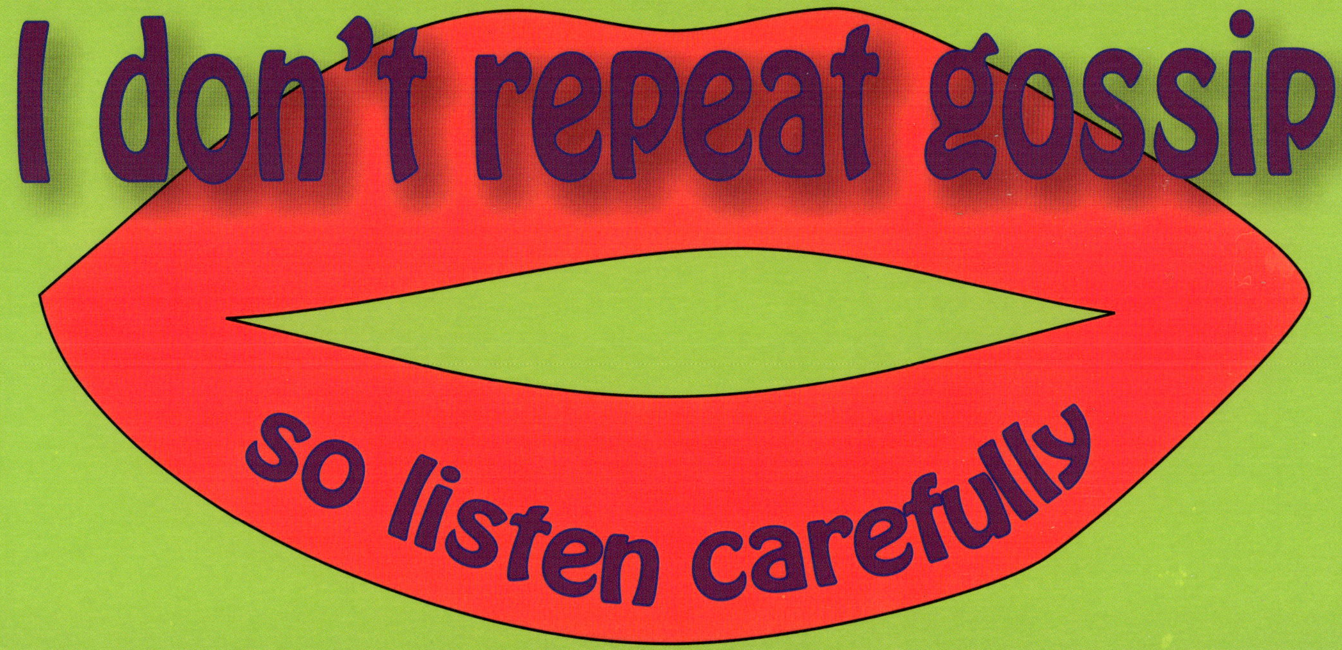
I don't repeat gossip
so listen carefully

Hello!
ANYBODY IN THERE?

EAGLES DON'T FLOCK

I'm nicer in person

you are free

TO DO AS I SAY

YOUR
JEDI MIND TRICKS
WON'T WORK ON ME